THE ONE AND
THE MANY IN THE
ISRAELITE CONCEPTION
OF GOD

By

AUBREY R. JOHNSON

CARDIFF
UNIVERSITY OF WALES PRESS
1961

FIRST EDITION 1942
SECOND EDITION 1961

PRINTED IN GREAT BRITAIN

PREFACE

THE regular requests which, much to my encouragement, the University of Wales Press continues to receive for a reissue of this work make it necessary for me to offer an apology for its being left out of print for so long. The fact is that I have been hoping to incorporate the argument of these pages in a longer monograph which should bear the title *The Holy One of Israel*; but, as I have to turn my attention for a while to the revision or completion of other monographs in this series, I have decided that I owe it to my many would-be readers to reproduce it for the time being in what is virtually its original form. This means that I have made only a few minor changes, whether in the body of the work or in the footnotes, and these changes are almost wholly confined to an attempt to bring the production as a whole into closer conformity with later monographs in the series—especially in what is to be their revised form. For the same reason this edition has been furnished with a set of indexes which corresponds to that in *Sacral Kingship in Ancient Israel*.

It will be clear from what I have already said that nothing has been done to bring the footnotes up to date; but, as I pointed out in a late addendum to the first edition, readers should consult J. P. Hyatt, *The Treatment of Final Vowels in Early Neo-Babylonian* (1941), in connexion with the argument of pages 26 f., although, as it seems to me, the two treatments of the features under consideration may be regarded as supplementary. In any case the general argument of my monograph remains quite unaffected.

Warm thanks are due to my friend and former pupil, the Reverend C. G. Williams, for his help in the reading of the proofs and in the checking of the indexes. I also take this opportunity of placing on record once again my sense of indebtedness to the University of Wales Press for undertaking the publication of my monographs and to the Oxford University Press for the care which is given so uniformly and so characteristically to their production.

AUBREY R. JOHNSON

Cardiff
June 1960

PRINCIPAL ABBREVIATIONS

A.f.O.	*Archiv für Orientforschung.*
B.Z.A.W.	Beihefte zur *Zeitschrift für die alttestamentliche Wissenschaft.*
C.A.H.	*The Cambridge Ancient History.*
C.B.	Cambridge Bible.
Cent.B.	The Century Bible.
E	The Elohistic narrative, or the Elohist.
E.T.	*The Expository Times.*
G.K.	Gesenius–Kautzsch, *Hebrew Grammar*, 2nd English edition, rev. by A. E. Cowley (1910).
H.K.	Handkommentar zum Alten Testament.
I.C.C.	The International Critical Commentary.
J	The Yahwistic narrative, or the Yahwist.
J.T.S.	*Journal of Theological Studies.*
K.A.T.	Kommentar zum Alten Testament.
LXX	The Septuagint.
P	The Priestly Code or School.
R.A.	*Revue d'assyriologie et d'archéologie orientale.*
R.B.	*Revue biblique.*
R.H.R.	*Revue de l'histoire des religions.*
S	The Syriac Version (Peshiṭta).
S.N.V.A.O. II.	Skrifter utgitt av Det Norske Videnskaps-Akademi i Oslo, II. Hist.-Filos. Klasse.
V	The Vulgate.
Z.A.W.	*Zeitschrift für die alttestamentliche Wissenschaft.*
Z.D.M.G.	*Zeitschrift der deutschen morgenländischen Gesellschaft.*

NOTE. Italics have been used in translations from Biblical and other texts in order to draw attention to certain words and phrases.

THE ONE AND THE MANY IN THE ISRAELITE CONCEPTION OF GOD[1]

FOR convenience of presentation this short study is divided into three parts with a major division between Part I and Parts II–III. In Part I there is offered a brief survey of the Israelite conception of man, and in Parts II–III this is used to attempt an elucidation of the Israelite conception of God.

The argument as a whole may be held to furnish yet another illustration of the general truth that psychology and theology move *pari passu*.[2]

I

The researches of P. (E.) Dhorme,[3] J. Pedersen,[4] and H. Wheeler Robinson[5] have revealed the fact that in Israelite thought psychical functions have a physical basis, and that man is conceived, not in some analytical fashion as 'soul'

[1] A paper originally read before the Society for Old Testament Study at Queens' College, Cambridge, on July 19th, 1939.

[2] Cf. the statement made by E. O. James and cited with approval by S. A. Cook to the effect that, in dealing with the question of 'monotheism', one must be prepared to take into consideration a 'psychological tendency'. E. O. James, 'A Comparative Study of the Old Testament in the Light of Recent Anthropological and Archaeological Research', in *A New Commentary on Holy Scripture*, ed. C. Gore, H. L. Goudge, and A. Guillaume, rev. edit. (1929), p. 673b; 'Primitive Monotheism', in *The Sociological Review*, xxvii (1935), p. 339. S. A. Cook, in a review of the first edition of the above-mentioned commentary, *J.T.S.* xxx (1928–9), p. 308; 'Primitive Monotheism', *J.T.S.* xxxiii (1931–2), p. 8. Cf., too, B. Balscheit's discussion of the psychological features of 'monotheism', in *Alter und Aufkommen des Monotheismus in der israelitischen Religion*, B.Z.A.W. 69 (1938), pp. 1–11.

[3] 'L'Emploi métaphorique des noms de parties du corps en hébreu et en accadien', *R.B.* xxix (1920), pp. 465–506; xxx (1921), pp. 374–99, 517–40; xxxi (1922), pp. 215–33, 489–517; xxxii (1923), pp. 185–212; reproduced in book form in 1923.

[4] *Israel: its Life and Culture I–II* (1926).

[5] e.g. in 'Hebrew Psychology', in *The People and the Book*, ed. A. S. Peake (1925), pp. 353 ff.

and 'body', but synthetically as a psychical whole. This is
commonly summed up by citing the J narrative of the
Creation, which tells how Yahweh first modelled a man out
of earth or clay and then breathed into the nostrils of this
figure, so that *it* 'became a living נֶפֶשׁ'.[1] In both the
Authorized and the Revised Versions נֶפֶשׁ is here rendered
by 'soul'; but this rendering is misleading if it suggests
any such dichotomy as that which finds early emphasis in
Orphic myth and Platonic philosophy.[2] The term נֶפֶשׁ is
obviously being used to indicate, not something conceived
as but one (albeit the superior) part of man's being, but
the complete personality as a unified manifestation of vital
power; it represents what Pedersen has called 'the grasping
of a totality'.[3]

What is more, this power is thought to reach far beyond
the mere contour of the body; and to denote this feature it
will be helpful to follow L. Lévy-Bruhl[4] in his use of a
telling expression from J. van Wing's study of the Bakongo.[5]
Thus one may say that man is thought to possess an indefinable 'extension' of the personality which enables him
to exercise a subtle influence for good or ill within the community. In its positive or beneficent aspect this power is
known as 'blessing', while in its negative or maleficent
aspect the extended personality makes its influence felt as
a 'curse'.[6]

In this way the spoken word may be regarded as an

[1] Gen. ii. 7 (J).
[2] Cf. Plato, *Cratylus*, 400 c; *Phaedo*, 64 c ff.: and see further, for example,
V. D. Macchioro, *From Orpheus to Paul* (1930), pp. 101 ff., 176 ff.
[3] Op. cit., pp. 106–33.
[4] *L'Âme primitive* (1927), p. 142, E.T. by L. A. Clare, *The 'Soul' of the
Primitive* (1928), pp. 121 f.
[5] *Études Bakongo* (1920), p. 129.
[6] Cf. Pedersen, op. cit., pp. 182 ff., 437 ff.; also *Der Eid bei den Semiten*
(1914), pp. 64 ff.; S. Mowinckel, *Psalmenstudien V. Segen und Fluch in
Israels Kult und Psalmdichtung*, S.N.V.A.O. II, 1923, No. 3 (1924), pp. 5 ff.,
61 ff.; J. Hempel, 'Die israelitischen Anschauungen von Segen und Fluch
im Lichte altorientalischer Parallelen', *Z.D.M.G.* lxxix (1925), pp. 20 ff.;
K. Hj. Fahlgren, *ṢeDĀḲĀ, nahestehende und entgegengesetzte Begriffe im
Alten Testament* (1932), pp. 158 ff.

effective 'extension' of the personality.[1] The obvious example is that of Isaac who, having once bestowed blessing upon Jacob, is unable to retract his words and nullify their effect in favour of the rightful recipient; once uttered they act creatively in quasi-material fashion.[2] Of course, as one learns from the same story, words vary in their range, so that it is not every word which may be regarded as a potent 'extension' of the personality; everything depends upon the occasion, the degree of vital power possessed by the speaker, and the extent to which, as the English idiom has it, he puts his 'soul' into what he says. Hence Isaac, having put his 'soul' into bestowing blessing upon Jacob, can only express what is practically a curse over Esau.

The value ascribed to the word as a potent 'extension' of the personality has a close parallel in the similar importance attached to the name;[3] and here we meet one of the most widespread, as it has been one of the most lasting, conceptions of this kind.[4] Thus to the Israelite, when the time comes for that dissolution of the personality which is known as death, it is in this particular 'extension' that he may continue to live most powerfully. Hence the extermination of the name is regarded as the greatest disaster which can befall a man, and various measures are adopted to preserve his memory. The need of male offspring for this particular purpose finds typical expression in the legislation providing for the so-called levirate marriage, which lays down that, if a man should die childless, his wife[5]

shall not marry without unto a stranger: her husband's brother shall go in unto her and take her to him for a wife and enter into a levirate marriage with her; and the first male child she beareth shall maintain the name of his dead brother, so that his name may not be wiped out of Israel.

[1] Cf., in general, M. A. Canney, *Givers of Life* (1923), pp. 53 ff.; G. van der Leeuw, *Phänomenologie der Religion* (1933), pp. 379 ff., E.T. by J. E. Turner, *Religion in Essence and Manifestation* (1938), pp. 403 ff.

[2] Gen. xxvii. 33 ff. (JE).

[3] Cf. Pedersen, *Israel: its Life and Culture I–II*, pp. 245 ff.

[4] Cf. Canney, op. cit., pp. 74 ff.; van der Leeuw, op. cit., pp. 129 ff., 266, E.T., pp. 147 ff., 287.   [5] Deut. xxv. 5 f.

For the same reason Absalom set up a pillar in the neighbourhood of Jerusalem, it being expressly said that he adopted this method because he had no (surviving?) son to perpetuate his name.[1] The same point of view is revealed by Bildad when he thus describes the ultimate fate of the wicked:[2]

> His memory doth perish from the earth;
>   He hath no name abroad.
> He is driven from light into darkness;
>   He is chased out of the world.
> He hath neither offspring nor progeny among his people;
>   There is no survivor where he dwelt.

The last point serves to introduce an aspect of the Israelite conception of man which is of the first importance for the present study. It recalls the fact that (in a way wholly in line with the grasping of a totality) a man's personality is thought of as extending throughout his בַּיִת, i.e. 'house' or 'household'. The father, of course, is the head; and next in order of importance are alternatively the wife (or wives) and the sons, then the sons' wives and the daughters.[3] As is clear from the case of Achan,[4] however, the strong solidarity felt to exist within such a social unit is also thought to extend to the whole of the property, so that the household in its entirety is regarded as a psychical whole—the extended personality of the man at its head.

One consequence of the importance attached in this way to members of one's household as 'extensions' of the personality may be seen in that feature of Hebrew style which points to what may be called an oscillation as between the conception of the אָדוֹן, the 'lord' or 'master' of the household, and that of a servant who (as such an 'extension' of his master's personality) acts as his agent, notably as a מַלְאָךְ or 'messenger'. A case in point is to be found

---

[1] 2 Sam. xviii. 18: cf. xiv. 27.
[2] Job xviii. 17 ff.
[3] e.g. Gen. vii. 1, 7 (J), 13 (P); or, again, xxxvi. 6 (P).
[4] Joshua vii. 24 f. (JE).

in the story of Joseph's dealings with his brethren in
Egypt: i.e.[1]

When they were gone out of the city, and were not yet far off,
Joseph said unto his steward, Up, follow after the men; and when
thou dost overtake them, say unto them, Wherefore have ye rewarded evil for good? Is not this it in which my lord drinketh, and
whereby he indeed divineth? Ye have done evil in so doing. And he
overtook them, and he spake unto them these words. And they said
unto him, Wherefore speaketh my lord such words as these? Far be
it from thy servants to do such a thing. Behold, the money, which
we found in our sacks' mouth, we brought again unto thee out of the
land of Canaan: how then should we steal out of thy lord's house
silver or gold? With whomsoever of thy servants it be found, let
him die, and we also will be *my lord's servants.*

The last reference, as one would expect and as the sequel
shows,[2] must virtually be to Joseph, although the words are
addressed to his steward; but the steward himself, as the
'extension' of his lord's personality, is able to say (in the
name of Joseph, so to speak):[3]

Now also let it be according unto your words: he with whom it is
found shall be *my* servant; and ye shall be blameless.

Through the agency of his steward Joseph is regarded as
being present—'in person'. In short, the מַלְאָךְ ('messenger'), as an 'extension' of his master's personality, not
merely represents but *is* virtually the אָדוֹן ('lord'). This
appears even more clearly, perhaps, in the following passage from the story of Jephthah:[4]

[1] Gen. xliv. 4 ff. (J). Note, too, that LXX reads: 'Joseph said unto his
steward, Up, follow after the men; and when thou dost overtake them, say
unto them, Wherefore have ye rewarded evil for good? *Wherefore have ye
stolen of me the silver cup?* Is not this it in which my lord drinketh?...' The
expression 'of me' may seem at first to refer to the steward rather than to
Joseph; but verse 2 ('my cup, the silver cup') suggests that the immediate
reference is to Joseph, and that as a result this is another example of the
oscillation under discussion.   [2] Verses 16 f.   [3] Verse 10.
[4] Judges xi. 12–13. Note, too, the rendering of V: 'Et misit nuntios ad regem
filiorum Ammon, qui *ex persona sua* dicerent: Quid mihi et tibi est, quia
venisti contra me ut vastares terram meam? Quibus ille respondit: Quia
tulit Israel terram meam quando ascendit de Aegypto, a finibus Arnon
usque Jaboc atque Jordanem; nunc ergo cum pace redde mihi eam.'

And *Jephthah sent messengers* (מַלְאָכִים) unto the king of the children of Ammon, saying, What have *I* to do with thee, that thou art come unto me to fight against my land? And the king of the children of Ammon answered *unto the messengers of Jephthah*: Because Israel took away my land, when he came out of Egypt, from Arnon unto the Jabbok as far as the Jordan; now therefore restore *thou* them peaceably.

Through the agency of his messengers Jephthah, like Joseph, is regarded as being present—'in person'. In other words, the מַלְאָכִים ('messengers'), as 'extensions' of their master's personality, are treated as actually *being* and not merely as representing their אָדוֹן ('lord').[1]

In the same way any part of a man's property is thought to form an 'extension' of the personality. Hence, when Elisha sent his servant Gehazi ahead with his staff, which was to be the particular instrument for restoring the Shunammite's son to life, he warned him against bestowing blessing upon anyone whom he might meet. In carrying the staff Gehazi would be bearing some of Elisha's forceful personality; and accordingly he was to preserve this power intact and not run the risk of weakening it, or even losing it altogether, by bestowing it rashly upon those for whom

[1] This point may be stressed as being of possible importance for textual and literary criticism. Cf., for example, Judges iii. 19: 'I have a secret message for thee, O king.' If these words were addressed to the king indirectly (i.e. through an attendant as an 'extension' of his personality), then it is not the case that this passage affords 'the most striking evidence' for the theory that the narrative in question is derived from a double source. Cf., for example, C. F. Burney, *The Book of Judges*, 2nd edit. (1920), p. 67. Similarly it will be recalled that in 2 Kings vi. 33 the term הַמַּלְאָךְ is usually altered to הַמֶּלֶךְ on the major ground that 'the verbs of *v.* 33b are only explicable if placed in the king's mouth' (C. F. Burney, *Notes on the Hebrew Text of the Books of Kings* (1903), p. 290). However, as the מַלְאָךְ would be regarded as an 'extension' of the king's personality, the words in question are wholly explicable as the text stands. Moreover, the proposed emendation only serves to create difficulty: cf. J. Skinner, Cent. B. (no date), *in loc.*

The oscillation under discussion, which is by no means peculiar to Israelite thinking but is to be found elsewhere in the ancient Semitic world, has already been recognized by F. Stier, *Gott und sein Engel im Alten Testament* (1934); but in view of the Israelite conception of man, as outlined above, one must beware of the too obvious assumption that such oscillation is to be explained in terms of a forgetfulness on the part of the writer.

it was not intended.¹ This instance, no doubt, is somewhat exceptional; but that is because Elisha was an exceptionally powerful person.² In varying degree the same principle holds good of any individual, so that the bestowal of a gift is nothing less than a sharing of one's personality. Thus a gift is sometimes called a 'blessing'—and inevitably so, for it involves a transference of one's vital power quite as much as, and perhaps more than, the spoken word. Accordingly, when Caleb's daughter said to her father, 'Prithee, give me a blessing!' he presented her with what appear to have been some wells or pools.³ On the same principle, when Achan selfishly violated the taboo which had been laid on the spoil taken at the capture of Jericho and thus brought what was virtually a curse upon the community, remedial measures to eradicate this poisonous sore from the social body were directed, not only against the figure of the im- mediate culprit, but also against his sons, daughters, oxen, asses, flocks, tent, and, in fact, 'all that he had'.⁴

Accordingly, in Israelite thought the individual, as a נֶפֶשׁ or centre of power capable of indefinite extension, is never a mere isolated unit; he lives in constant reaction towards others. Moreover, the latter fall into two classes, those with whom he is close-knit within the sphere of the social unit as his extended or larger 'self' and those who are outside this sphere:⁵ and here again one may see evidence of the grasping of totality, for from first to last in the work of those different schools of thought which did so much to mould the Hebrew Scriptures the conception of the social

---

¹ 2 Kings iv. 29: cf. Pedersen, op. cit., p. 201. Of course, it is usual to hold the more immediately obvious view that 'the object of the injunction is to avoid the waste of time involved in the formal and tedious salutations customary in the East'. Skinner, op. cit., *in loc.* Nevertheless Pedersen's interpretation, although it may seem forced and unnatural at first, appears quite natural and straightforward when it is seen against that general back- ground of Semitic thought which finds ready illustration in, say, E. Wester- marck's account of the Moorish conception of *baraka*, i.e. 'blessing', in *Ritual and Belief in Morocco* (1926), i, pp. 35–261.   ² Cf. 2 Kings ii. 9 ff.
³ Judges i. 14 f.; cf. Joshua xv. 18 f. (J).   ⁴ Joshua vii. 24 (JE).
⁵ Cf. W. Robertson Smith, *The Religion of the Semites*, 3rd edit. with notes by S. A. Cook (1927), p. 272.

unit is dominated by that of kinship; it governs alike the treatment of general history, as represented by the context of the patriarchal narratives, and that of the particular story of Israel.

The nucleus of the social unit or kin-group is the household, which (as already observed) is a psychical whole representing the extended personality of the man at its head. Nevertheless, kinship extends far beyond the borders of the household; and wherever it is recognized there is the recognition of a psychical whole. This fact has been made familiar in the works of S. A. Cook,[1] H. Wheeler Robinson,[2] and J. Pedersen;[3] but it is so important for the development of the writer's thesis that certain outstanding features must be recalled.[4] To continue therefore: the social unit or kin-group, however widely conceived, is a single נֶפֶשׁ or 'person'—albeit what H. Wheeler Robinson has designated a 'corporate personality'.[2] Thus the dissatisfaction of the Israelites during the period of the Wandering is expressed by saying that the נֶפֶשׁ[5] of this people grew impatient; and they are represented as voicing their impatience thus: 'Our נֶפֶשׁ is sick of this cursed food!'[6] Examples of this kind, which may be multiplied,[7] serve to explain the fact that any association of individuals suggestive of homogeneity, such as Jehu's confederate circle,[8] a set of infidels,[9] or even (as there will be occasion to notice again later) the Baby-

---

[1] In *C.A.H.* iii (1925), pp. 437 ff.; in W. Robertson Smith, op. cit., pp. 503 ff., 590 ff., 655 ff.; also *The Old Testament: a Reinterpretation* (1936), pp. 115 ff.

[2] See above, p. 1, n. 5; also 'The Hebrew Conception of Corporate Personality', in *Werden und Wesen des Alten Testaments*, ed. J. Hempel, B.Z.A.W. 66 (1936), pp. 49 ff.

[3] See above, p. 1, n. 4.

[4] For the sake of brevity the fact that such extension occurs, so to speak, in time as well as in space is ignored in what follows; but this is an important point which may not be omitted in a fuller treatment of the subject. Cf. O. Eissfeldt, *Der Gottesknecht bei Deuterojesaja* (1933), E.T. in *E.T.* xliv (1932–3), pp. 261 ff.; S. A. Cook, op. cit., pp. 118 f.; J. Hempel, *Das Ethos des Alten Testaments*, B.Z.A.W. 67 (1938), pp. 41 ff.   [5] N.B. singular *not* plural.

[6] Num. xxi. 4 f. (JE); cf. xi. 6 (JE).

[7] e.g. Gen. xxiii. 8 (P); Isa. iii. 9; Ps. cxxiv. 7.

[8] 2 Kings ix. 15.   [9] Isa. lxvi. 3.

Ionian pantheon,[1] may be treated as a kin-group forming a single נֶפֶשׁ or corporate personality.

In much the same way it is said of the Israelites that, after their forces had been put to flight at Ai, their heart[2] melted and became like water.[3] Similarly, it is said of David that, having appealed for the loyalty of the people of Judah on the ground of kinship as represented by common bone and flesh, he 'bent the heart[2] of all the menfolk of Judah as it were one man'.[4]

This conception of the social unit or kin-group as a corporate personality finds particularly vivid expression, however, in a passage which, though dealing with a Philistine city, obviously reflects the Israelite point of view. In this connexion it will be recalled that, after the Philistines had captured the Ark, they found it exercising a disastrous influence in their midst; and accordingly it was sent from city to city as anything but a welcome guest. Ultimately it came to Ekron; and the Hebrew narrative picturesquely records the ensuing consternation as follows:[5]

When the Ark of God came to Ekron, the Ekronites cried out, saying: The Ark of the God of Israel has been brought around to *me* to slay *me* and *my* kin. They therefore sent and gathered together all the rulers of the Philistines, and said: Send away the Ark of the God of Israel; let it return to its proper place, so that it may not bring death to *me* and *my* kin.

Here the city as forming a kin-group is clearly represented as a corporate personality, and such a vivid instance enables one to understand how an Israelite city, such as that of Abel, could be known as 'a mother in Israel'.[6]

Again, in the story of the Israelite wanderings for example, one finds a similar conception of the social unit on a somewhat more extended scale, as when one reads:[7]

And the Canaanite (the king of Arad) who dwelt in the Negeb heard that Israel came by the way of (the) Atharim; and he fought

---

[1] Isa. xlvi. 2.   [2] N.B. singular *not* plural.   [3] Joshua vii. 5 (JE).
[4] 2 Sam. xix. 15 (EVV. 14).
[5] 1 Sam. v. 10 f.   [6] 2 Sam. xx. 19.   [7] Num. xxi. 1–3 (JE).

against Israel, and took of *him* captive. And Israel vowed a vow unto
Yahweh, and said, If Thou wilt indeed deliver this people into *my*
hand, then *I* will devote their cities. And Yahweh hearkened to the
voice of Israel, and delivered up the Canaanite, and *he* devoted them
and their cities.

In the light of such examples one can understand the
attractiveness of the theory (so liable to over-emphasis)
that 'the narratives of Genesis present us, not with real,
historical personages, but with personifications'.[1] So, too,
it is little wonder that the attempt has been made to interpret the 'I' of many of the Psalms in terms of such collective
units.[2]

Further, it may be noticed in passing that this point of
view is not peculiar to the Hebrew records; it appears also
in the Tell el-Amarna tablets in a letter sent by the city of
Irḳata to the Pharaoh, thus:[3]

This tablet is the tablet of Irḳata.[4] To the king, our lord, thus
(saith) Irḳata and the people of her . . . (?): At the feet of the king,
our lord, seven times seven times do we fall. To our lord, the sun,
thus (saith) Irḳata: Let the heart of the king, the lord, know that
we guard Irḳata for h(i)m.

.   .   .   .   .

May the king, our lord, hearken to the words of his faithful servants,
and give a present to his servant, while our enemies look on and eat
dust!

The parallel with the foregoing passages from the Hebrew
records is so close that this letter might not seem to require
further comment. Nevertheless the tablet is of additional
interest in that it introduces another aspect of the concep-

[1] A. Kuenen, *The Religion of Israel to the Fall of the Jewish State*, trans.
A. H. May, i (1882), p. 111.

[2] Cf. R. Smend, 'Ueber das Ich der Psalmen', *Z.A.W.* viii (1888),
pp. 49–147.

[3] Lines 1–10, 31–36. Text in C. Bezold and E. A. Wallis Budge, *The Tell
el-Amarna Tablets in the British Museum* (1892), No. 42, pp. 86 f. and
Plate 4. Transliteration and translation in J. A. Knudtzon, *Die El-Amarna-
Tafeln* (1915), No. 100, pp. 450 ff.; and in S. A. B. Mercer, *The Tell el-
Amarna Tablets* (1939), No. 100, pp. 338 ff.

[4] It should be pointed out, perhaps, that the name Irḳata is preceded by
the determinative for 'city'.

tion of the social unit which is of the first importance in the present connexion. This appears in the last sentence given above, i.e.:

May the king, our lord, hearken to the words of his faithful *servants*, and give a present to his *servant*, while our enemies look on and eat dust!

Here there is obvious indication of an oscillation in the mind of the writer according as he thinks of the social unit in question as an association of individuals (and thus uses the plural 'servants') or as a corporate personality (and thus uses the singular 'servant'[1]); and such oscillation with regard to the social unit may frequently be found in Israelite thought. This appears most clearly, perhaps, in the colourful account of the Israelites' attempt to pass through Edom on their way to the Promised Land. It runs thus:[2]

And Moses sent messengers from Kadesh to the king of Edom: Thus saith thy brother Israel. Thou knowest all the trouble that hath befallen us: how our fathers went down to Egypt, and we dwelt in Egypt many days, and the Egyptians maltreated us and our fathers; and when we cried unto Yahweh, He heard our voice, and sent a Messenger (*or* Angel), and brought us forth out of Egypt; and, behold, we are in Kadesh, a city on the border of thy territory. Prithee, let us pass through thy land. We will not pass through field or through vineyard; neither will we drink well-water. We will go along the king's way; we will not turn aside to the right hand nor to the left, until we pass through thy territory. And Edom said to him: Thou shalt not pass through me, lest I come out with the sword against thee. And the children of Israel said unto him: *We will go up by the highway; and, if we drink thy water, I and my cattle, then I will give the price thereof: only ('tis nothing!) let me pass through on*

---

[1] It is interesting to observe that Mercer ignores this oscillation, and offers a uniform translation by rendering the singular in both instances.

[2] Num. xx. 14–21 (JE). Careful attention should be paid to the whole passage, not merely to the single sentence italicized in the text. Note, too, the way in which Israel's message is sent by means of מַלְאָכִים, who preface what they have to say with 'Thus saith . . .'. Cf. the conception of the prophet as the מַלְאָךְ of Yahweh, as discussed below, pp. 32 ff. Attention may also be drawn to the fact that the messengers disappear from the scene, so to speak, leaving the stage to the major contestants, Israel and Edom. This agrees with the similar feature already observed in the case of what we should call an individual as distinct from a corporate personality: see above, p. 6, n. 1.

my feet. And he said: Thou shalt not pass through. And Edom came
out to meet him with a weighty company and with a strong hand.
Thus Edom refused to allow Israel to pass through his territory,
and Israel turned away without troubling him further (*lit.* from
upon him).

Here the oscillation in thought between the conception of
the social unit as an association of individuals (with the
resultant use of plural forms) and as a corporate personality
(with the consequent use of the singular) is unmistakable.
Of course, we sometimes betray a similar oscillation when
we have occasion, for example, to think of a committee;
but our thinking is not so dominated by this point of view
as that of the Israelites seems to have been. The Book of
Deuteronomy, for instance, is completely under its sway;[1]
and, when once this is recognized, one sees how precarious
were the attempts of, say, W. Staerk[2] and C. Steuernagel[3]
to carry through an analysis of this book based in large
measure upon the fluctuations between the singular and the
plural modes of address.[4] Indeed one cannot but be concerned at the possibility of going astray in textual as well
as literary criticism through a desire to secure a 'logical'
coherence often foreign to Israelite thinking.[5] So far as
textual criticism is concerned this is a very real danger in
the case of the Psalter, where, as H. Wheeler Robinson has
pointed out,[6] such oscillation or fluidity of reference as we
have been noticing is of frequent occurrence.[7] Finally, both

[1] Cf., for example, Deut. xxix. 1–5 (EVV. 2–6); and see below, pp. 34 f.

[2] *Das Deuteronomium. Sein Inhalt und seine literarische Form* (1894).

[3] *Der Rahmen des Deuteronomium* (1894); *Die Entstehung des deutero-
nomischen Gesetzes* (1896); H.K. (1898), 2nd edit. rev. (1923).

[4] Cf., in criticism of such attempts, E. König, K.A.T. (1917), pp. 21 ff.;
George Adam Smith, C.B. (1918), pp. lxxiii–lxxxviii.

[5] See above, p. 6, n. 1; and cf. A. Guillaume, *Prophecy and Divination*
(1938), pp. 54 f.   [6] e.g., op. cit., pp. 57 f.

[7] Cf. Ps. lxxxi, where the apparent confusion of the text is really due, not
merely to oscillation as between the individual and the corporate unit, but
also to that fluidity of movement within the prophetic consciousness to
which attention is drawn below, pp. 33 ff. (It should be pointed out that the
phrase 'fluidity of movement', although used here in a different context, is
derived from H. Wheeler Robinson, loc. cit.)

H. Wheeler Robinson[1] and O. Eissfeldt[2] have made valuable use of this conception to help elucidate the problem offered by the figure of the Servant of Yahweh in Isaiah xl–lv.

So, to sum up (with an emphasis upon the 'extensions' of the personality), we may say of the Israelite conception of man that it was so diffuse that Heraclitus might well have been speaking in Hebrew rather than Greek terms when he said:[3]

Though thou shouldst traverse every path, thou couldst not discover the boundaries of 'soul'; it hath so deep a meaning.

II

In conformity with the view, approved by the Priestly School, that man was made in the image of God,[4] we may now apply something of what we know concerning the Israelite conception of man to an elucidation of the corresponding conception of God.

In the earliest portions of the Hebrew Scriptures, notably in the J narrative (as in the story of the Creation[5] or the extraordinary account of the revelation of the divine Figure to Moses[6]), Yahweh is conceived in strongly anthropomorphic fashion; and this has its counterpart in those continued anthropopathic references, in which psychical functions of an emotional, volitional, or an intellectual kind are ascribed to Yahweh, as when He is said to be compassionate and merciful,[7] to love[8] and to hate,[9] to be angry[10]—and so on.[11] We must notice at once, however, a distinction of

[1] Op. cit., pp. 58 ff.; and *The Cross of the Servant* (1926).

[2] See p. 8, n. 4.

[3] H. Diels, *Die Fragmente der Vorsokratiker*, 4th edit. (1922), i, p. 86 (No. 45); cf. van der Leeuw, op. cit., p. 254, E.T., p. 275.

[4] Gen. i. 26 f. (P).   [5] Gen. ii. 4b ff. (J).

[6] Exod. xxxiii. 12–23 (J).   [7] e.g. Exod. xxxiv. 6 (J); Ps. lxxxvi. 15.

[8] e.g. 2 Sam. xii. 24; Hos. iii. 1, xi. 1.

[9] e.g. Amos vi. 8; Hos. ix. 15; Jer. xii. 8.

[10] e.g. Exod. iv. 14 (J); 2 Sam. vi. 7.

[11] For a recent appreciation of these anthropopathic references in so far as they may be held to throw light on the prophetic consciousness of ancient Israel, see A. Heschel, *Die Prophetie* (1936).

the first importance between the conception of man and that
of God: for we may not say of the latter (as was said of the
former) that psychical functions have a physical basis; or,
at least, we may not do this and, at the same time, give the
term 'physical' the same content in each case. Thus even
in the earliest records Yahweh, though undoubtedly pic-
tured in the form of a man, was nevertheless thought of as
a Being of a different substance from the latter. In fact, it
seems that He was normally conceived (as Ezekiel explicitly
describes Him in virtue of his own experience[1]) in terms of
a light and rarefied substance best explained as 'like fire';
and one may compare those chariots and horses of fire
which appear in the Elisha stories as the instruments of
Yahweh's will.[2] The point of view is summed up for us,
of course, in Isaiah's well-known oracle against those of his
fellow-countrymen who looked to Egypt for help against
Assyria:[3]

> Woe
>> To them that go down to Egypt for help,
>>> And on horses would depend,
>> And trust in chariots, for they are many,
>>> And in horsemen, for they are very strong;
>> And they have not looked to the Holy One of Israel,
>>> Yea, Yahweh they have not sought!
>
>>   .   .   .   .   .
>
>> The Egyptians are men and not God,
>>> And their horses are flesh and not spirit (רוּחַ).

The distinction is here made explicit;[4] for the parallelism,
coupled with the foregoing illustrations, will surely warrant
our saying that Yahweh, like the heavenly forces under
His control, differs from mankind as being of a more
rarefied substance 'like fire'—in short, רוּחַ or 'Spirit', a

----

[1] i. 26 f.   [2] 2 Kings ii. 11 f.; vi. 17.   [3] xxxi. 1–3.
[4] Cf. Gen. vi. 3 (J); Jer. xvii. 5; Ps. lvi. 5 (EVV. 4): and see further Pedersen, op. cit., pp. 176 f.; H. Wheeler Robinson, *The Christian Experience of
the Holy Spirit* (1928), pp. 10 ff. The statement made in the text should
perhaps be qualified to this extent that 'it is never said that this substance
was *ruach*, yet it belongs to the realm of *ruach*'. (H. W. R., loc. cit.)

term which is reserved in the case of man (at least in the early period) to describe the more vigorous manifestations of life on his part, especially such as might be attributed to the influence of the Godhead.[1] This being the case (and provided that we are careful to define our terms), we must say that, so far as the conception of God was concerned, psychical functions had a 'spiritual' rather than a physical basis.

However, this is not all; for here we may remind ourselves that in Israelite thought, while man was conceived, not in some analytical fashion as 'soul' and 'body', but synthetically as a psychical whole and a unit of vital power, this power was found to reach far beyond the contour of the body and to make itself felt through indefinable 'extensions' of the personality. Now the same idea is quite clearly present in the conception of the Godhead—notably, in the first place, in this very notion comprehended by the term רוּחַ. We have already touched upon the fact that any manifestation of unusual vigour which marked a man out as an exceptionally powerful personality, such as the resolution of Gideon,[2] the prowess of Samson,[3] the infectious behaviour of the early prophets,[4] or the qualities of a firm ruler,[5] might be attributed to the influence of the רוּחַ (as the 'Spirit') of Yahweh; but, clearly, such examples must be understood in terms of the 'Spirit' as an 'Extension' of Yahweh's Personality. Thus, even in such cases as those in which the רוּחַ of Yahweh is said to have 'donned' Gideon (like a garment)[6] or to have 'rushed' upon Samson[7] or upon Saul,[8] it may hardly be said to have been regarded as an

---

[1] Cf. H. Wheeler Robinson, in *The People and the Book*, pp. 358 ff.

[2] Judges vi. 34.   [3] Judges xiv. 6, 19; xv. 14.

[4] 1 Sam. x. 5–13; xix. 18–24.   [5] Isa. xi. 2.

[6] Judges vi. 34. The Hebrew term should be compared, not only with the cognate Syriac forms which are used to denote demoniacal and other possession (cf. G. F. Moore, I.C.C. (1895), *in loc.*), but also with the cognate Arabic مَلْبُوس, as used, for example, with reference to the frenzy of the dervishes. Cf. E. W. Lane, *The Manners and Customs of the Modern Egyptians*, 5th edit. (1860), in the Everyman's Library edition, pp. 455 f.

[7] Judges xiv. 6, 19; xv. 14.   [8] 1 Sam. x. 10.

impersonal force. This is important in view of the fact
that, as H. Wheeler Robinson has pointed out,[1] there is
only one certain instance in the Hebrew Scriptures in which
the רוּחַ is *clearly* personalized. The instance in question is
that of the רוּחַ who, in Micaiah's vision, proposed to be
a lying or deceptive 'spirit' in the mouth of all Ahab's
prophets.[2] In the light of the Israelite conception of man,
however, it would seem that this רוּחַ, as a member of
Yahweh's heavenly Court (or 'Household'!), should be
thought of as an individualization within the corporate רוּחַ
or 'Spirit' of Yahweh's extended Personality;[3] in other
words, that we must be prepared to recognize for the Godhead just such fluidity of reference from the One to the
Many or from the Many to the One as we have already
noticed in the case of man.

This should become clearer as we proceed. Meantime,
for the sake of completeness in pursuing the main argument
of these pages, it is to be observed that (as is already obvious
from the conception of the רוּחַ) God is thought of in terms
similar to those of man as possessing an indefinable extension of the Personality which enables Him to exercise a
mysterious influence upon mankind. In its creative aspect
this appears as 'blessing'; in its destructive aspect it makes
itself felt as a 'curse'.[4]

[1] *The Christian Experience of the Holy Spirit*, p. 9; as against P. Volz,
*Der Geist Gottes und die verwandten Erscheinungen im Alten Testament und
im anschliessenden Judentum* (1910), pp. 2 ff.   [2] 1 Kings xxii. 19 ff.
[3] Thus, despite the criticism by E. Bevan, *Symbolism and Belief* (1938),
pp. 163 f., there seems to be some justification for the treatment of this passage by F. Büchsel, *Der Geist Gottes im Neuen Testament* (1926), pp. 3 ff.
Cf., too, the well-known fact that 'the conception of the indwelling Spirit
is in Paul hardly separable from the conception of the living Christ' (C. H.
Dodd, *History and the Gospel* (1938), p. 56). Paul here reveals himself as a
true son of Israel; and Dodd is right in rejecting the view that this feature
of Paul's thinking involves 'a certain depersonalizing of the idea of Christ'
(H. J. Holtzmann, *Lehrbuch der neutestamentlichen Theologie*, 2nd edit. rev.
(1911), ii, p. 88). The full implication of this reference to Paul should become
clearer as the reader continues. Meantime the bearing of this whole point
upon the problems raised by the New Testament conception (*or* conceptions)
of the 'Spirit' will be apparent to any informed reader.
[4] See above, p. 2, n. 6.

Thus it is that (again as in the case of man) the 'Word' may be regarded as a potent 'Extension' of Yahweh's Personality.[1] Not to spend too much time upon this point, we may remind ourselves of the familiar passage:[2]

> As the rain cometh down
>> And the snow from heaven,
> And returneth not thither,
>> But watereth the earth,
> And maketh it bring forth and bud,
>> That it may give seed to the sower and bread to the eater,
> So shall My 'Word' be that goeth forth out of My Mouth;
>> It shall not return unto Me void,
> But it shall perform that which I please,
> And succeed in that whereto I sent it.

These lines reflect that primitive and widespread conception of the power of the spoken word which lies behind so many magical practices;[3] and there is good reason to believe that, so far as the prophets in general were concerned, this conception was often something more than mere poetical imagery. In fact, it is wholly in line with those magical ideas which have rightly been recognized as lying behind their so-called symbolism.[4] The 'Word' (דָּבָר) is one with the 'thing' (דָּבָר) which is to be performed;[5] it has objective reality, and thus forms a powerful 'Extension' of the divine Personality.

In the same way the 'Name'[6] is an important 'Extension' of Yahweh's Personality analogous to that which is observable in the case of man. Thus it is that a knowledge of the 'Name' is a matter of ritual importance, as is clear from

[1] Cf. O. Grether, *Name und Wort Gottes im Alten Testament*, B.Z.A.W. 64 (1934), pp. 59 ff.; L. Dürr, *Die Wertung des göttlichen Wortes im Alten Testament und im antiken Orient* (1938).

[2] Isa. lv. 10 f.

[3] Cf. van der Leeuw, op. cit., pp. 379 ff., E.T., pp. 403 ff.

[4] Cf. H. Wheeler Robinson, 'Prophetic Symbolism', in *Old Testament Essays* (1927), pp. 1 ff.

[5] Cf. 1 Sam. iii. 11; Ezek. xii. 21–28.

[6] Cf. Grether, op. cit., pp. 1 ff.; also G. F. Moore, *Judaism in the First Centuries of the Christian Era, The Age of the Tannaim*, i (1927), pp. 423 ff.

its use in the official priestly blessing, as preserved in the P Code:[1]

> Yahweh bless thee, and keep thee!
> Yahweh make His Face to shine upon thee, and be gracious unto thee!
> Yahweh lift up His Face toward thee, and grant thee peace!

Yahweh's emphatic comment upon this, as recorded by the P Code, is to be noted:

So, when they (i.e. the priests) put My 'Name' upon the children of Israel, then 'tis *I* (וַאֲנִי) will bless them.

A similar emphasis upon the divine 'Name' occurs more than once in the Psalter; for example, in a short liturgical composition which probably comes from the circle of the cultic prophets:[2]

> May Yahweh answer thee in the day of distress!
>   May the 'Name' of the God of Jacob make thee prevail!
> May He send thy help from the sanctuary,
>   And from Zion support thee!
> May He be mindful of all thy gifts,
>   And find thy burnt offerings acceptable!
> May He grant thee according to thy heart,
>   And fulfil thine every plan!
> May we rejoice in thy salvation (*or* victory),
>   And triumph through the 'Name' of our God!
> May Yahweh fulfil all thy requests!
>
> Now do I know that
>   Yahweh hath granted His Messiah salvation (*or* victory).
> He doth answer him from His holy heaven
>   By the mighty saving deeds of His Right Hand.

---

[1] See Num. vi. 22–27 (P).

[2] Ps. xx: cf. Ps. liv. For the possible connexion with the cultic prophets, see the writer's article, 'The Prophet in Israelite Worship', *E.T.* xlvii (1935–6), pp. 317 f. Observe, too, the further fluidity of thought in the last line (cf. p. 12, nn. 5 and 7), revealed by the transition from the 2nd to the 3rd person; and note that, in such a context as the above, it marks the obscurity of the border-line between spell and prayer which is such a feature of the Psalter: cf., for example, Pss. xii and xxviii. Accordingly, to follow LXX and emend the text for the sake of uniformity (as the writer originally did, loc. cit., in common with most editors) now seems highly questionable.

These invoke chariots, and these invoke horses;
But we invoke the 'Name' of Yahweh our God.
The former are bowed down and fallen;
But we are risen and set on our feet.

O Yahweh, grant the king salvation (*or* victory)!
May He answer us on the day that we call!

Thus it is that the phrase 'to call with (EVV. "upon", i.e. בְּ) the Name "Yahweh" ' is the technical expression for denoting cultic observances.[1] So, too, one can understand why the Deuteronomic Code lays recurrent emphasis upon the sanctuary as 'the place which Yahweh thy God shall choose to put His "Name" there' or 'the place which Yahweh your God shall choose to let His "Name" dwell there'.[2]

Enough has been said to illustrate the close parallel between the Israelite conception of man and that of God so far as the immediately obvious 'extensions' of the personality are concerned. Our study of the conception of man, however, revealed a belief in other 'extensions' of the personality which were of a much wider character. We found, for instance, that a man's property was thought of in this way, as in the somewhat extreme example furnished by the story of Elisha's sending his staff in the charge of his servant Gehazi as the means of restoring the Shunammite's son to life. Elisha warned Gehazi against greeting (that is, bestowing blessing upon) anyone whom he might meet; for, in carrying the staff, Gehazi would be bearing some of Elisha's forceful personality, and therefore he was to preserve this power intact and not run the risk of weakening it, or even losing it altogether, by distributing it thoughtlessly amongst those for whom it was not intended.[3] As already remarked, this instance is somewhat exceptional; but that is because Elisha was an exceptionally powerful person. There is all the more reason, therefore, to cite this in illustration of the role played by the Ark, for example, as a further 'Extension' of Yahweh's extraordinarily powerful Personality. Thus,

[1] Gen. iv. 26, xii. 8, and often in J; Zeph. iii. 9.
[2] e.g. Deut. xii. 5, 11, 21.   [3] See above, p. 7, n. 1.

apparently prior to being carried into battle, the Ark was addressed in quite personal fashion as follows:[1]

> Arise, Yahweh, that Thine enemies may be scattered,
> That they that hate Thee may flee before Thee!

Similarly, on its return, it was hailed with the cry:

> Return, Yahweh, unto the ten thousand families of Israel!

Further, we read that, when the Israelites had sent to Shiloh for the Ark after their defeat by the Philistines at Aphek, and[2]

the Ark of the Covenant of Yahweh came into the camp, all Israel shouted with a great shout, so that the earth rang again. And when the Philistines heard the sound of the shouting, they said, What meaneth the sound of this great shouting in the camp of the Hebrews? Then they knew that the Ark of Yahweh had come into the camp. And the Philistines were afraid, for they said, *God* (or *A God*) *is come* (בָּא אֱלֹהִים) into the camp. And they said, Woe unto us! For there hath not been such a thing before. Woe unto us! Who shall deliver us out of *the Hand of these mighty Gods* (מִיַּד הָאֱלֹהִים הָאַדִּירִים הָאֵלֶּה)? *These are the Gods that smote* (אֵלֶּה הֵם הָאֱלֹהִים הַמַּכִּים) the Egyptians with every kind of blow in the wilderness.

Here the Ark is again identified with Yahweh—whether the reference be to a 'God' or to 'Gods' (and this is a point to which we shall return). Moreover, despite the capture of the Ark on the occasion under discussion, the potency of this obvious 'Extension' of Yahweh's Personality appears clearly enough in the ensuing story of its (*or* His?) adventures in the land of the Philistines, as at Ekron for example,[3] and may be illustrated further by reference to the incident at Bethshemesh on its (*or* His?) return journey to Israelite territory, when it (*or* He?) provoked the cry:[4]

> Who is able to stand before Yahweh, this Holy God, and to whom can He (*or* it?) go up so as not to trouble us further (*lit.* from upon us)?

Our discussion of this point, however, may best be brought to a close by reverting to the account of the instructions

---

[1] Num. x. 35 f. (JE?): cf. G. B. Gray, I.C.C. (1903), *in loc.*; see also Ps. lxviii. 2 (EVV. 1).   [2] 1 Sam. iv. 5-8.
[3] See above, p. 9, n. 5.   [4] 1 Sam. vi. 20.

given by the Philistines' priests and diviners for getting rid of this menace, as it offers a clear example of what is for us the ambiguity of reference as between the Ark and Yahweh, i.e.:[1]

> Now therefore take and prepare you a new cart and two milch kine, on which there hath come no yoke, and tie the kine to the cart, and bring their calves home from them: and take the Ark of Yahweh, and lay it upon the cart; and put the articles of gold, which ye return Him as a reparation, in a coffer beside it, and send it away, that it may go. And see, if it goeth by the way of its own border to Beth-shemesh, then 'tis He hath done us this great evil: but if not, then we shall know that it is not His Hand that smote us; it was an accident that happened to us.

In the sequel, of course, the cattle (wholly contrary to instinct and lowing reluctantly) are compelled to travel farther and farther away from their calves, thus revealing the power inherent in the Ark, which is again virtually indistinguishable from Yahweh;[2] so that in the last sentence, for example, one might equally well render the Hebrew by

> If *He* goeth by the way of *His* own border

as by

> If *it* goeth by the way of *its* own border.

Indeed the territorial reference makes the former the more probable.

In considering the Israelite conception of man, however, we found that (in a way wholly in line with that grasping of a totality which is characteristic of Israelite thinking) a man's personality was thought of as extending throughout his 'household'; and that, indeed, the conception of the individual may not be dissociated from that of his kin-group (conceived in ever-widening circles of relationship) —with a resultant oscillation in thought as between the individual, the kin-group conceived as an association of individuals, and the kin-group thought of in vivid fashion as a single unit or corporate personality. Now our study of

[1] 1 Sam. vi. 7-9.
[2] Cf. H. P. Smith, I.C.C. (1899), *in loc.*

the conception of man and that of God has thus far revealed
so close a parallel between the two, notably in the ever-
widening character of the 'Extensions' of the Personality,
that one seems driven to ask the question (which, indeed,
has already arisen in connexion with our discussion of the
רוּחַ or 'Spirit' of Yahweh) as to whether we should not
take the further step in consideration of the Godhead, and
be prepared to recognize possible traces of that very wide
'Extension' of the Personality which would embrace the
social unit—conceived either as an association of what we
should call individuals or as a corporate personality.

III

There seems to be no gainsaying the fact that at one time
in Israel (as indeed in the Jewish colony at Elephantine so
late as the fifth century B.C.[1]) Yahweh was worshipped as a
member, albeit the chief member, of a Pantheon. We may
cite, for example, the various references to בְּנֵי הָאֱלֹהִים
or the בְּנֵי אֵלִים, in which the use of the term בֵּן is akin
to that in בְּנֵי הַנְּבִיאִים and simply denotes a kin-group.[2]
Thus the J Code preserves a legend of marriages between
the 'Sons of God' (*or* 'Sons of the Gods': בְּנֵי הָאֱלֹהִים)
and the 'Daughters of Man' (*or* 'Daughters of Men': בְּנוֹת
הָאָדָם);[3] and the prologue to the Book of Job gives us a
picture (not unlike that in Micaiah's vision) of the heavenly
Court or divine Assembly, at which the 'Sons of God' or
'Sons of the Gods' or, simply, 'Gods' are said to present
themselves before Yahweh.[4] It is against such a background
that one should see the בְּנֵי אֵלִים referred to in the Psalter:[5]

> Give to Yahweh, ye Gods (בְּנֵי אֵלִים),
> Give to Yahweh glory and strength;
> Give to Yahweh the glory due to His Name:
> Bow down to Yahweh in holy array.

---

[1] Cf. A. Cowley, *Aramaic Papyri of the Fifth Century B.C.* (1923),
pp. xviii ff.; A. Vincent, *La Religion des Judéo-Araméens d'Éléphantine*
(1937), pp. 100 and 562 ff.   [2] Cf. Pedersen, op. cit., pp. 53 f.
[3] Gen. vi. 1–4.   [4] i. 6, ii. 1.   [5] Pss. xxix. 1–2, lxxxix. 7–8 (EVV. 6–7).

Who in the clouds doth equal Yahweh,
 Is like Yahweh among the Gods (בְּנֵי אֵלִים),
A God (אֵל) Who is terrible in the Council of the Holy Ones,
 Greater and more dread than all those about Him?

In the circumstances it is not surprising that difficulty should
sometimes be occasioned over what is for us the ambiguity
inherent in the use of the plural form אֱלֹהִים.[1] We have
already noticed one instance of such apparent ambiguity,
i.e. in the account of the entry of the Ark into the camp of
the Israelites during their struggle with the Philistines.[2]
Another example is afforded by the close of Psalm lviii, i.e.:[3]

The righteous shall rejoice when he seeth the vengeance:
 He shall wash his feet in the blood of the wicked.
So that men shall say, Verily there is a reward for the righteous:
 Verily there is a God that judgeth in the earth.

This translation follows the rendering of the Revised Ver-
sion; but, as a matter of fact, the Hebrew of the last line is
(for us) quite ambiguous; it may equally well be rendered:

So that man shall say, Verily there is a reward for the righteous:
 Verily there are Gods that judge in the earth.

The ambiguity of reference in the case of this term appears
again in the polemic of the Deuteronomic School against
the worship of 'other gods' (אֱלֹהִים אֲחֵרִים) than Yahweh; i.e. in the following statement, where the expression
אֱלֹהֵיהֶם must have (for us) a plural significance in that it
refers back to those 'other gods' whose worship is con-
demned earlier in the passage:[4]

And thou shalt consume all the peoples which Yahweh thy God
shall deliver unto thee; thine eye shall not pity them: neither shalt
thou serve their *gods* (אֱלֹהֵיהֶם); for *he* is a snare unto thee (כִּי־
מוֹקֵשׁ הוּא לָךְ).

[1] Since this paper was given the writer has found that, in much of what he
has to say with regard to the oscillation in the conception of אֱלֹהִים and the
comparison with the Accadian ILÂNI, he was anticipated more than a quarter
of a century ago by J. Hehn, *Die biblische und die babylonische Gottesidee*
(1913), pp. 175 ff.   [2] See above, p. 20, n. 2.
[3] Verses 11–12 (EVV. 10–11).
[4] Deut. vii. 16: cf. Exod. xxiii. 33 (where the readings of the Ancient
Versions should also be compared with the M.T.).

The oscillation as between plural and singular which occurs
here, for all that it is obscured by the English as by the
Ancient Versions, is wholly in line with that which we
observed in the account of the entry of the Ark into the
Israelite camp; and that the passage is indeed to be taken
in this sense seems to be confirmed by the similar tendency
to oscillation displayed everywhere by the Deuteronomic
Code in its references to man.[1]

At this stage it is appropriate to draw attention to the
Accadian plural ILĀNI which, like אֱלֹהִים, appears to be
capable of a singular reference. This seems to be the case,
for example, in the Tell el-Amarna letters, where (besides
being construed in at least one instance with a singular
verb[2]) it frequently appears in the form ILĀNI-IA as a mode
of address to the Pharaoh, e.g.:[3]

To the king, my sun, my god (ILI-IA), my god(s) (ILĀNI-IA), thus
(saith) Abimilki thy servant.

In such a context ILĀNI certainly seems to have a singular
implication.[4]

Further, the terms אֱלֹהִים and ILĀNI, besides their ambiguity of reference, have a very wide connotation. Thus
the former may be used of the spirits of the dead, as in the
story of Saul's consultation of Samuel through the agency
of the witch of En-dor, where it is used with a singular
reference;[5] or again, as in Isaiah's polemic against necromancy, where (apparently in quoting the argument of his op-
ponents) he seems to use the term with a plural reference, i.e.:[6]

Consult the ghosts and the familiar spirits that chirp and mutter.
Should not a people consult its אֱלֹהִים—on behalf of the living, the
dead (הַמֵּתִים)?

[1] See above, p. 12, n. 1.
[2] Knudtzon, No. 96; Mercer, No. 96; lines 4–6. Text in O. Schroeder,
Die Tontafeln von el-Amarna (1915), No. 49.
[3] Bezold, No. 30; Knudtzon, No. 151; Mercer, No. 151; lines 1–2.
[4] Cf. the quotation given below, p. 26, n. 1, in which ILĀNI is construed
with a singular participle.
[5] 1 Sam. xxviii. 13; but note the plural participle עֹלִים.
[6] viii. 19: see further G. B. Gray, I.C.C. (1912), *in loc.*

Similarly the term ILĀNI is used with very wide reference; it embraces not only the 'gods' proper (with their strongly marked individual traits) but also demons of the vaguest kind; and here one may quote (from the series of bilingual magical texts which bore the name UTUKKI LIMNŪTI, i.e. 'The Evil Spirits') an incantation directed against the SIBIT ILĀNI, i.e. the 'Seven':[1]

> Destructive storms and evil winds are they,
> An evil blast that heraldeth (*lit.* beholdeth) the baneful storm,
> An evil blast, forerunner of the baneful storm.
> They are mighty children, mighty sons.
> Heralds of the pestilence are they.
> Throne-bearers of Ninkigal are they.
> They are the flood which rusheth through the land.
> Seven gods of the broad heaven,
> Seven gods of the broad earth,
> Seven robber gods are they,
> Seven gods of might,
> Seven evil gods,
> Seven evil demons,
> Seven evil demons of oppression,
> Seven in heaven and seven on earth.

The term 'Seven' in such a context seems to be used vaguely with reference to an innumerable host, and one may compare the name 'Legion' borne by the 'unclean spirit' of whom we read in the story of the demoniac healed by Jesus in the country of the Gerasenes. Indeed this story is of further interest in the present connexion, for it reveals that as late as the first century of the Christian era such demons were thought of in a quite vague and indeterminate way with a resultant oscillation as between the one and the many. Thus we read:[2]

And when he saw Jesus from afar, he ran and worshipped him;

---

[1] Text in *Cuneiform Texts from Babylonian Tablets, &c.*, *in the British Museum* xvi, Tablet v, col. ii. 65–iii. 26 (plates xiii and xiv); transliteration and translation in R. Campbell Thompson, *The Devils and Evil Spirits of Babylonia*, i (1903), pp. 62 ff., which is followed here save in one small point.

[2] Mark v. 6 ff.: cf. i. 23 ff. Cf., too, such contemporary oscillation in the conception of man as survives in Matt. xxiii. 37: 'O Jerusalem, Jerusalem,

and crying out with a loud voice, he saith, What have I to do with
thee, Jesus, thou Son of the Most High God? I adjure thee by God,
torment me not. For he said unto him, Come forth, *thou unclean
spirit*, out of the man. And he asked him, What is *thy* name? And
he saith unto him, *My* name is Legion; for *we* are many. And *he*
besought him much that he would not send *them* away out of the
country. Now there was there on the mountain side a great herd of
swine feeding. And *they* besought him, saying, Send *us* into the
swine, that *we* may enter into them. And he gave *them* leave. And
the unclean spirits came out, and entered into the swine.

Comment is needless. It is therefore interesting to find a
similar oscillation in the conception of the SIBIT ILĀNI,
when, as actually happened, these attained to the status of
a deity of the first rank.[1] A clear example is to be found in
the record of a treaty effected in the seventh century B.C.
between Baʻal of Tyre and Esarhaddon of Assyria, in which
various Assyrian and Phoenician deities are invoked in
ratification of the agreement.[2] The line which immediately
concerns us is as follows:[3]

(ilu) SI-BIT-TE ILĀNI ḲAR-DU-TE INA
(iṣu) KAKKÊ-ŠU-NU (?)-KU-NU LIŠ-KUN

To reproduce the effect of the oscillation under discussion
this may be rendered:

As for Sibitti, the mighty god(s), may *he* bring about your (over-
throw?) with *their* weapons!

The fluidity of reference as between the one and the many
in the case of this (*or* these) ILĀNI is obvious.

which killeth the prophets, and stoneth them that are sent unto her! How
often would I have gathered *thy* children together, even as a hen gathereth
her chickens under her wings; and *ye* would not!'

[1] Cf. H. C. Rawlinson, *The Cuneiform Inscriptions of Western Asia* (1870–
91) iv, plate 21, No. 1 (B), Rev. 9 ff., e.g. 22: God(s) Seven, destroyer of the
wicked! (ILĀNI SI-BIT MU-ḪAL-LIḲ LIM-NU-TI). Cf. H. Zimmern, *Beiträge zur
Kenntnis der babylonischen Religion* (1896–1901), pp. 168 f., for transliteration and translation; and see further M. Jastrow, *Die Religion Babyloniens
und Assyriens*, i (1905), pp. 173 ff., 387 ff.

[2] For the text see S. Langdon, 'A Phoenician Treaty of Assarhaddon',
R.A. xxvi (1929), pp. 189 ff.; and, for a transliteration and translation, see
E. F. Weidner, *A.f.O.* viii (1932–3), pp. 29 ff.   [3] Rev. ii. 5.

However, there is another point of interest in this tablet to which attention must be drawn, for later we read:[1]

May the great gods of heaven and earth, the gods of Assyria, the gods of Accad, the gods of the land beyond the River, curse you with an indissoluble curse! As for Baʿal-sameme, Baʿal-malagê, Baʿal-ṣapunu, may *he* raise an evil wind against *their* own ships! May *he* loosen the rigging thereof! May *they* tear out the mast thereof!

Here, in the fact that the Baʿal-sameme (Baʿal of Heaven), the Baʿal-malagê (Baʿal of Kings—or Messengers, i.e. 'Angels'?),[2] and the Baʿal-ṣapunu (Baʿal Ṣaphon) may be construed as either singular or plural, we have evidence of what we may call a triune Baʿal[3]—a deity who is both three in one and one in three. The Babylonian pantheon, we may recall,[4] could be thought of in Hebrew as a kin-group forming a single נֶפֶשׁ or corporate personality.

All in all, therefore, it would seem that, when we find an oscillation as between the One and the Many in the Israelite conception of Yahweh, we should be prepared to interpret it in this light. We have already touched upon the evidence for a Pantheon in the thought of early Israel; so that this point may be concluded by simply referring to such passages as:[5]

And Yahweh God said, Behold, the man is become *as one of Us*, to know good and evil.

And Yahweh came down to see the city and the tower, which the children of men built. And Yahweh said, Behold, they are one people, and they have all one language; and this is what they begin to do: and now nothing will be withholden from them, which they purpose to do. Go to, let *Us* go down, and let *Us* there confound their language.

And I heard the voice of the Lord saying: Whom shall *I* send, and who will go for *Us*?

[1] Rev. ii. 8 ff. The reference to 'their (own) ships' is commonly misunderstood, as by Weidner who takes it to be a scribal error for 'your ships'.
[2] The form 'malagê' may be an Aramaism: cf. E. Dhorme, *L'Évolution religieuse d'Israël*, i (1937), pp. 326 f., who takes it thus in the former sense.
[3] Cf. Dhorme, loc. cit.   [4] See above, p. 9, n. 1.
[5] Gen. iii. 22 (J), xi. 5 ff. (J); Isa. vi. 8. (Note the oscillation with reference to the people in the ensuing oracle.) The suggestion that the plural which occurs in these passages may be one of 'majesty' is rightly rejected in G.K. § 124*g*, n. 2.

In the circumstances does not such fluidity of reference
seem best explained in terms of that oscillation as between
the one and the many which we have seen to be characteristic of the Israelite conception of man and also present
on occasion in, say, the Assyrian conception of deity?[1] In
short, may one not suggest with a degree of probability
that any Israelite who thought his אֱלֹהִים to be Many also
thought his אֱלֹהִים to be One?

However, we may not leave the matter there, as another
feature of Israelite thought concerning the Godhead calls
for elucidation along these lines. In fact it serves to reinforce
what has been said concerning this oscillation as between
the One and the Many in the Israelite conception of God.
The feature in question is the conception of the 'Angel' or
'Messenger' (מַלְאָךְ) of Yahweh,[2] which has a double significance, according as this agent, *qua* individual, belongs to
the class אֵל or אֱלֹהִים or to the class אָדָם.

The apparently human figure with whom Jacob is said
to have struggled at the ford of the Jabbok (i.e. at Penuel:
פְּנוּאֵל) is afterwards recognized by him as (an) אֱלֹהִים;[3]
and Hosea, in referring to this incident, says of Jacob:[4]

> In the womb he took his brother by the heel;
> In his strength he strove with God (*or* a God: אֱלֹהִים):

[1] Of course one must be prepared to recognize that such a form of speech
may have come to be used ultimately as a mere matter of idiom, and may
then have lost its original force. Accordingly one hesitates to express an
opinion on such a passage as that from the Priestly Code in Gen. i. 26 f.:
'And God said, Let *Us* make man in *Our* image, after *Our* likeness; . . . And
God created man in *His* own image.' Again, how is one to explain the
oscillation which is so characteristic of the Koran? Is it enough to say that
this is 'merely' idiomatic or stylistic? Cf., for example, Sura ii. 149 ff., which
offers an instance of oscillation in the conception of man and in that of Allah.

[2] Cf. A. Lods, 'L'Ange de Yahvé et "l'âme extérieure" ', in *Studien zur
semitischen Philologie und Religionsgeschichte* (J. Wellhausen *Festschrift*), ed.
K. Marti, B.Z.A.W. 27 (1914), pp. 263–78: and esp. F. Stier, op. cit. (see
above, p. 6, n. 1). One hesitates to say anything suggesting an adverse
criticism of so thorough and painstaking a piece of work, but it seems to the
writer that Stier's treatment of the subject is too analytical, and suffers from
a failure to fit the material into the context of the general Israelite conception
of personality, human and divine.

[3] Gen. xxxii. 23–32 (E).   [4] xii. 4 f. (EVV. 3 f.).

Yea, he strove against an 'Angel' (מַלְאָךְ) and prevailed;
He wept and made supplication to him.

Now it is commonly regarded as an extraordinary feature of the conception of the מַלְאָךְ יהוה (and, therefore, one worthy of special comment) that he is frequently indistinguishable from Yahweh Himself;[1] but the reason for this is now clear. It is but another aspect of that oscillation as between the individual and the corporate unit within the conception of God which we have been studying; and it has its parallel in the fact that in the conception of man the human מַלְאָךְ or 'messenger' may be similarly indistinguishable from the human אָדוֹן or 'lord'.[2] In illustration of this point it will be sufficient to cite several passages, offering partial quotation from what are rather long narratives but leaving the phraseology, on the whole, to speak for itself.

Genesis xvi. 7–14 (J), e.g. 7–10, 13a:

And *the 'Angel' of Yahweh* found her by a fountain of water in the wilderness, by the fountain on the way to Shur. And he said, Hagar, Sarai's handmaid, whence camest thou, and whither goest thou? And she said, I flee from the face of my mistress Sarai. And *the 'Angel' of Yahweh* said unto her, Return to thy mistress, and submit thyself under her hands. And *the 'Angel' of Yahweh* said unto her, *I* will greatly multiply thy seed, that it shall not be numbered for multitude. . . . And she called the Name of *Yahweh Who had spoken unto her* . . . .

Here we have an oscillation as between Yahweh and, apparently, a *single* מַלְאָךְ or 'Messenger' who is virtually indistinguishable from Him.

Judges vi. 11–24, e.g. 11–13a, 14:

And *the 'Angel' of Yahweh* came, and sat under the terebinth which was in Ophrah, that pertained unto Joash the Abiezrite: and his son Gideon was beating out wheat in the winepress, hiding from the Midianites. And *the 'Angel' of Yahweh* appeared unto him, and said unto him, Yahweh is with thee, thou mighty man of valour.

[1] For a summary of the attempted explanations, see Stier, op. cit., pp. 1 ff.
[2] See above, p. 6, n. 1.

And Gideon said unto him, O my lord, if Yahweh be with us, why then is all this befallen us? . . . And *Yahweh* turned to him, and said, Go in this thy might, and save Israel from the hand of Midian: have not *I* sent thee?

The sequel shows that it is still the 'Angel' of Yahweh speaking with Gideon; so that once again we have evidence of the fact that the 'Angel' or 'Messenger' of the class אֱלֹהִים is indistinguishable from Him. As already remarked, this in itself is well known; but we are now in a position to see that this is wholly in line with Israelite thinking. Hence it need be no matter for surprise that the 'Angel', as thus indistinguishable from Yahweh, may also be thought of in terms of the One and the Many. At least, the recognition of such a point seems to offer a solution of the difficulties commonly felt on reading, say:

Genesis xviii–xix (J), e.g. xviii. 1–5, 9–10a:

And *Yahweh* appeared unto him by the terebinths of Mamre, as he sat in the entrance of the tent during the heat of the day. And he lifted up his eyes and looked, and, lo, *three men* stood over against him: and when he saw them, he ran towards them from the entrance of the tent, and bowed down to the earth, and said, My lord (*or* My lords), if now I have found favour in *thine* eyes, prithee, pass *thou* not on from *thy* servant. Let now a little water be fetched, and wash *ye your* feet, and rest *you* under the tree. And I will fetch a morsel of bread, and sustain *ye your heart*; after that *ye* shall pass on. Inasmuch as *ye* have come to *your* servant! And *they* said, So do, as thou hast said. . . . And *they* said unto him, Where is Sarah thy wife? And he said, Lo, in the tent. And *He* said, *I* will certainly return unto thee when the time cometh round; and, lo, Sarah thy wife shall have a son . . . .

Here we have an oscillation as between Yahweh and at least *two*, perhaps *three*, 'Angels' or 'Messengers'; for in the sequel Abraham's visitors are designated as such;[1] and, further, there is an oscillation as between the singular and plural forms of reference, so that it is not clear whether the singular is a singular of individualization or that of a collective unit. Of recent years the attempt has been made to

[1] xix. 1, 15.

explain this apparent confusion either in terms of a fusion
of sources or in terms of an editorial expansion (imperfectly
carried through!) which is thought to point to a growing
transcendence in the conception of God;[1] but we have
already had occasion to note the misleading effect of trying
to impose upon the Hebrew Scriptures what one thinks is a
more 'logical' coherence.[2] It is therefore possible that the
same point of view, involving the One and the Many in the
conception of the 'Angel' of Yahweh, finds expression in
the words of the psalmist, when he says:[3]

> The 'Angel' of Yahweh *encampeth* (חֹנֶה)
> *Round about* them that fear Him, and ,delivereth them.

Of course it may be held that the psalmist, in referring thus
to the מַלְאַךְ יהוה, has in mind an individual as the com-
mander of the heavenly forces; but in the light of Israelite
thinking as a whole this may be doubted. One may compare
(in conjunction with the frequent use of, say, אִישׁ יִשְׂרָאֵל
in a corporate sense[4]) the illuminating passage:[5]

> Now Jacob had gone on his way, and there met him 'Angels' of
> God (*or* 'Messengers' of Gods: i.e. מַלְאֲכֵי אֱלֹהִים). And Jacob said
> when he saw them, This is God's Host (*or* a Host of Gods: i.e.
> מַחֲנֵה אֱלֹהִים): and he called the name of that place Mahanaim
> (מַחֲנַיִם).

Against such a background it seems likely that, when the
psalmist speaks of the 'Angel' of Yahweh as *encamping
round about* those that fear Him, he has in mind a collective
unit or corporate personality; and that the reference is not
to what one may perhaps call a mere individual, or even
two or three such, but to a *host*.

We observed somewhat earlier, however, that the conception of the 'Angel' or 'Messenger' (מַלְאָךְ) of Yahweh
has what we should call a double significance according as

---

[1] Cf., for example, the discussion in H. Gunkel, H.K., 3rd edit. rev. (1910),
pp. 186 f., 194 f., and in Stier, op. cit., pp. 6 f.
[2] See above, p. 12, n. 5.   [3] Ps. xxxiv. 8 (EVV. 7).
[4] e.g. Judges xx. 11, 20; 2 Sam. xv. 13.   [5] Gen. xxxii. 2-3 (EVV. 1-2)(E).

the agent in question belongs to what we may describe as the celestial or the terrestrial order; and something of the apparent confusion which could result from this is to be seen in the story of the birth of Samson:

Judges xiii, e.g. 2 f., 6, 8 f., 20–22:

> And there was a man of Zorah, of the clan of the Danites, whose name was Manoah; and his wife was barren, and bare not. And *the 'Angel' of Yahweh* appeared unto the woman, and said unto her, Behold, now, thou art barren, and bearest not: but thou shalt conceive, and bear a son. . . . And the woman came and told her husband, saying, *A* (or *The*) *man of God* came unto me, and his appearance was like the appearance of *the* (or *an*) *'Angel' of God*, very terrible! . . . Then Manoah intreated Yahweh, and said, O Lord, prithee, let *the man of God* whom Thou didst send come again to us, and teach us what we shall do unto the child that shall be born. And God hearkened to the voice of Manoah, and *the 'Angel' of God* came again unto the woman as she sat in the field.

Thus far in the narrative the visitor is evidently thought to be no more than a 'man of God' (otherwise known as a 'prophet'[1]) of an exceptionally striking kind. It is only the sequel which shows him to have been of the celestial rather than the terrestrial order:

> And it came to pass, when the flame went up towards heaven from off the altar, that *the 'Angel' of Yahweh* ascended in the flame of the altar: and Manoah and his wife looked on; and they fell on their faces to the ground. But *the 'Angel' of Yahweh* did no more appear to Manoah or to his wife. Then Manoah knew that he was *the 'Angel' of Yahweh*. And Manoah said to his wife, We shall surely die, because we have seen *God* (or *a God*).

Accordingly it was possible for Yahweh Himself or His 'Angel' (indistinguishable from 'God' or 'a God') to be taken for 'a man of God' or 'prophet'.

Thus we reach our final point, which may be taken as the converse of this: i.e. that the prophet was commonly thought of as the מַלְאָךְ ('Messenger') of Yahweh *par excellence*, and might himself be virtually indistinguishable

---

[1] Cf. 1 Kings xiii.

from Him in certain circumstances. The background to this is furnished by Jeremiah in his polemic against the cultic prophets of his day; for, speaking in the Name of Yahweh, he says:[1]

> I have not sent the prophets;
>   Yet they ran.
> I have not spoken unto them;
>   Yet they have prophesied.
> If they had really stood in My intimate Council,
>   And had declared My 'Words' to My folk,
> They would have turned them back from their evil way
>   And from their evil practices.

The true prophet, then, was the 'Messenger' (מַלְאָךְ) of Yahweh;[2] he was a member of His intimate Council. Moreover (if the argument of these pages as to the Israelite conception of personality, human and divine, is sound), the prophet, in functioning, was held to be more than Yahweh's 'representative'; for the time being he was an active 'Extension' of Yahweh's Personality and, as such, *was* Yahweh— 'in Person'.[3] Of course, this is not to restrict Yahweh's human agents (so to speak) to this class. Were we to follow this treatment out to its conclusion, we should have to deal with such figures as those of the king,[4] the priest[5]—or any member of society as the 'Servant' of God.[6]

For confirmation of the point at issue we may turn to that form of an oscillation in the utterances of the prophets which suggests that the personality (on what we may call its human side) has been absorbed, as it were, in that of the Godhead; the prophet has become temporarily, at least, an important 'Extension' of Yahweh's Personality. *Mutatis mutandis*, this may be regarded as the converse of H.

---

[1] xxiii. 21 f.   [2] Cf. Hag. i. 13.   [3] Cf. pp. 4 ff.
[4] Cf. the writer's essay, 'The Rôle of the King in the Jerusalem Cultus', in *The Labyrinth. Further Studies in the Relation between Myth and Ritual in the Ancient World*, ed. S. H. Hooke (1935), pp. 71–111.
[5] Cf. Mal. ii. 7: and see further G. B. Gray, *Sacrifice in the Old Testament: Its Theory and Practice* (1925), pp. 219 ff.
[6] Cf. p. 13, nn. 1 and 2.

Wheeler Robinson's statement that 'there is a Godward, as well as a manward, application of corporate personality'.[1] It is a matter of polarity; and, as we are dealing now with the conception of God rather than that of man, we have to say in this context that there is a manward, as well as a Godward, application of corporate personality. Again we may quote two or three examples and leave them, for the most part, to speak for themselves.

Our first illustration is taken from outside the works of the canonical prophets, although the passage in question is ascribed to one who was regarded, perhaps, as the greatest of the prophets.[2] This passage is of special interest, although by no means unique, for it not only illustrates the oscillation which is here under discussion, but also combines with this an example of oscillation as between the one and the many in the conception of man. It is therefore reproduced twice, with varying emphasis upon the two types of oscillation.

Deuteronomy xxix. 1–5 (EVV. 2–6):

And Moses called unto all *Israel*, and said unto *them*: *Ye* have seen all that Yahweh did before *your* eyes in the land of Egypt unto Pharaoh, and unto all his servants, and unto all his land; the great trials which *thine* eyes saw, the signs, and those great wonders: but Yahweh hath not given *you* an heart to know, and eyes to see, and ears to hear, until this day. Yea, I have led *you* forty years in the wilderness: *your* clothes are not waxen old upon *you*, and *thy* shoe is not waxen old upon *thy* foot. *Ye* have not eaten bread, neither have *ye* drunk wine and strong drink—that *ye* might know that I, Yahweh, am *your* God.

Such oscillation as between the singular and the plural in the case of Israel is specially interesting in view of the equally striking oscillation effected by the speaker as he

[1] 'The Psychology and Metaphysic of "Thus saith Yahweh" ', *Z.A.W.* xli (1923), p. 10. Cf. the further statement, *in loc.*: 'To those who could conceive the merging of the individual in the family and the clan and the nation it must have been much easier for man's personality to be conceived as temporarily merged in that of God.'

[2] Cf. Deut. xviii. 15, xxxiv. 10; Hos. xii. 14 (EVV. 13).

passes from an objective 3rd Person to a subjective 1st Person in the case of Yahweh, thus:

And Moses called unto all Israel, and said unto them: Ye have seen all that *Yahweh* did before your eyes in the land of Egypt unto Pharaoh, and unto all his servants, and unto all his land; the great trials which thine eyes saw, the signs, and those great wonders: but *Yahweh* hath not given you an heart to know, and eyes to see, and ears to hear, until this day. Yea, *I* have led you forty years in the wilderness (*Who is to be held as speaking now? Is it still Moses in his own person—or is it Moses 'in the Person of' Yahweh?*): your clothes are not waxen old upon you, and thy shoe is not waxen old upon thy foot. Ye have not eaten bread, neither have ye drunk wine and strong drink—that ye might know that *I, Yahweh*, am your God.

The remaining illustrations are taken from the works of the canonical prophets themselves.

Isaiah xxii. 15 ff.:

15. Thus saith the Lord, Yahweh of Hosts:
    Go, get thee to this minister,
    To Shebna, who is over the house,
    (Saying:)
16. What hast thou here, and whom hast thou here,
    That thou hast hewn thee here a tomb?
    Hewing on high his tomb,
    Cutting him out an abode in the cliff!
17. Lo, *Yahweh* is about to hurl thee,
    Hurling, O man, and speeding, speeding thee on!
18. *He* will send thee spinning, spinning,
    Like a ball, to a land of wide expanse.
    There shalt thou die, and there shall be
    Thy glorious chariots, O shame to the house of thy lord!
19. Yea, *I* will thrust thee from thy post,
    And from thy station shall *He* pull thee down!

This passage affords another example of the unnecessary difficulty occasioned by that misleading anxiety to secure a more 'logical' coherence to which attention has already been drawn.[1] The change from 3rd Person to 1st Person

[1] See above, p. 12, n. 5, and p. 31, n. 2: and cf. the discussion in G. B. Gray, I.C.C. (1912), and O. Procksch, K.A.T. (1930), *in loc.*

in verses 17–18 and 19a, for example, finds ready explanation along the line indicated,[1] while the oscillation in verse 19 may be held to mark the transition to the regular use of the 1st Person in the remainder of the passage.[2]

Jeremiah ix. 1 f. (EVV. 2 f.):

> Oh that I had in the wilderness
> A wayfarer's lodge,
> That I might leave my people,
> That I might go from them!
> For they are all adulterers,
> A company of traitors!
> Yea, they have bent their tongue
> (Their bow!) deceitfully,
> And 'tis not through fidelity
> That they are strong in the land;
> Nay, 'tis from evil to evil that they proceed,
> And Me they know not—Oracle of Yahweh!

Here Jeremiah obviously begins in his own person; but in the last stichos he is equally clearly speaking 'in the Person of' Yahweh—reinforcing what he has to say by means of that frequent ejaculation on the lips of the prophets, 'Oracle of Yahweh!' Accordingly, any suggestion that this frequent ejaculation should be excised (on the ground, say, that it interferes with the metre or breaks into the message[3]) should be received with caution; for any seemingly unsystematic use of this kind may be governed by the urgent necessity of making it clear to listeners that the words

[1] Note, too, the different type of oscillation in verse 16; for this adds force to the above emphasis upon the type of oscillation under discussion.

[2] Of course the change of person in this case *may* be explained in terms of the use of the 3rd person with reference to an indefinite subject: cf. G.K. § 144 *de*. In any case there is no more justification for 'restoring' the 1st person in verse 19b on the ground that this is supported by V and S than there would be for citing LXX and V (as against S!) for reading the 2nd person instead of the 3rd person in verse 16cd.

[3] Cf., for example, P. Volz, K.A.T., 2nd edit. (1928), pp. xlviii f. and *in loc.* with reference to such a passage as Jer. xxiii. 30:

> Therefore, behold, I am against the prophets
> (Oracle of Yahweh!)
> Who steal My 'Words' from one another!

uttered are not (as might otherwise appear) the prophet's own but those of Yahweh Himself. It is Yahweh speaking —'in Person'.

If the argument of this short study is sound, we have here a point of view which needs to be borne in mind as an aid to the solution of, not only textual and literary problems, but even more those problems which are associated with the attempt to employ such terms as 'polytheism' and 'monotheism' in connexion with Israelite thought, and also those which are inherent in the question of the prophetic psychology or, again, that of revelation. It may also be argued that along this line we gain a new approach to the New Testament extension of Jewish Monotheism in the direction of the later Trinitarianism. This is apparent already in Part II, i.e. in the discussion of the 'Spirit'; and it may be held to come out even more clearly in Part III. At any rate, we can see how it was possible for a Jewish Christian to relate his Messiah so closely with the divine Being as to afford a basis for the later (and Greek) metaphysical formulation of the doctrine of the Trinity.[1] In conclusion, one may add that in a sense we seem to have come full circle; so that once again we may say of Heraclitus that he might well have been speaking in Hebrew rather than Greek terms when he said:

Though thou shouldst traverse every path, thou couldst not discover the boundaries of 'soul'; it hath so deep a meaning.

[1] The correlative to this, provided by the Godward application of corporate personality, is the Pauline conception of the individual believer as a man 'in Christ' and of the community of believers as the 'Body' of Christ. Cf. H. Wheeler Robinson, *The Cross of the Servant*, pp. 75 ff.

INDEX

(a) SUBJECTS

Where relevant page numbers apply to both text and footnotes.

Heraclitus, 13, 37.
Holy One, 23; of Israel, 14.
Hosea, 28.
Household, 4, 8, 21; heavenly, 16.

Infidels, set of, 8.
Irḳata, 10.
Isaac, 3.
Isaiah, 14, 24.
Israel, Israelite, 3, 6, 8 ff., 11 f., 16 n., 20, 22 f., 27 f., 34 f.

Jabbok, 6, 28.
Jacob, 3, 18, 28, 31.
Jehu, 8.
Jephthah, 5 f.
Jeremiah, 33, 36.
Jericho, 7.
Jerusalem, 4, 25 n.
Jesus, *see* Christ.
Joash the Abiezrite, 29.
Job, Book of, 22.
Jordan, 6.
Joseph, 5 f.
Judah, 9.

Kadesh, 11.
King, 18 f., 33.
Kin-group, kinship, 7 ff., 21 f., 27.
Koran, 28 n.

'Legion', *see* Spirit, spirits.
Levirate marriage, 3.
Logical coherence, 12, 31, 35.
Lord: divine, 28 ff.; human, 4 ff.

Magic, 17, 25.
Mahanaim, 31.
Mamre, 30.
Manoah, 32.
Master, *see* Lord.
Memory, 3 f.
Messenger, 4 ff., 27, 28 ff. *See also* Yahweh.
Messiah, 37. *See also* King.
Micaiah, 16, 22.
Midian, Midianites, 29 f.
Monotheism, 1 n., 37.
Moses, 11, 13, 34 f.
Most High: as appellation of God, 26.
Mother in Israel, 9.

Name, 3 f., 17 ff., 33. *See also* Yahweh.

Necromancy, 24.
Negeb, 9.
Ninkigal, 25.

Ophrah, 29.
Oracle, *see* Yahweh.
Orphic myth, 2.
Oscillation in thought, 4 ff., 11 f., 16, 18 n., 21, 23 f., 25 ff., 28 ff., 33 ff.

Pantheon, 22, 27 f.; Babylonian, 8 f., 27.
Patriarchal narratives, 8.
Paul, 16 n., 37 n.
Penuel, 28.
Personality: forceful or powerful, 6, 20 f.; corporate, 8 f., 11 f., 16, 21 f., 27, 29, 31, 33 f., 37 n.; dissolution of the, 3; extension of the, 2 f., 4 ff., 7 f., 13, 15 ff., 19 ff., 33 ff.
Personalization, 16.
Personification, 10.
Pharaoh, 10, 24, 34 f.
Philistines, 9, 20 f., 23.
Phoenicia, Phoenician, 26.
Platonic philosophy, 2.
Plural of majesty, 27 n.
Polarity, 34.
Polytheism, 37.
Possession, demoniacal and other, 15 n. *See also* Demons.
Power, vital, 2 f., 6 f., 15, 17, 19, 21.
Prayer, 18 n.
Priest, 18, 21, 33.
Priestly Code (or School), 13, 18, 28 n.
Property, 4, 6 f., 19.
Prophet, 15 ff., 25 n., 33 ff.; cultic, 18, 33; as man of God, 32; as messenger of Yahweh, 11 n., 31 ff.
Prophetic consciousness, 12 n., 13 n.
Prophetic psychology, 37.
Psalms, Psalter, 10, 12, 18, 22.
Psychical functions, 1 f., 13 ff.
Psychical whole, 2, 4, 8, 15.
Psychological tendency, 1 n.

Revelation, 37.
Righteous, 23.
River, the, *see* Euphrates.
Ruler, 15.

Samson, 15, 32.
Samuel, 24.

Subjects

INDEX

(b) AUTHORS

Page numbers usually refer to the footnotes.

INDEX

(c) SCRIPTURE REFERENCES

Where relevant page numbers apply to both text and footnotes.

All Old Testament references are to the Hebrew Text.

INDEX

(d) SELECT HEBREW WORDS AND PHRASES

Where relevant page numbers apply to both text and footnotes.

PRINTED IN GREAT BRITAIN
AT THE UNIVERSITY PRESS, OXFORD
BY VIVIAN RIDLER
PRINTER TO THE UNIVERSITY